THE TABERNACLE
WORKBOOK

A companion piece for the Tabernacle Video

Ray Neu

©Antioch Interactive, Inc. 2000

Contents

Introduction..2

Approaches to Study 3

Sanctuary..4

Dwell..6

Entrance 8

Altar...10

Wash..12

Sacrifice 14

Blood..16

Examine the Evidence..18

Acknowledge Your Need...19

Holy Place...20

Lampstand..22

Light...24

Bread..26

Incense...28

Curtain...30

Most Holy Place...32

Priests..34

Covenant..37

Presence...39

Quick Reference..44

Answer Key...45

The Tabernacle Workbook

A Companion Study for The Tabernacle Video

The Tabernacle is one of the most significant concepts in the Bible. Physically, it was a tent used for worship by the Israelites as they wandered in the wilderness. More importantly, however, the Tabernacle represented a focal point for increased spiritual understanding. It presented a plan of redemption that foreshadowed the coming of Jesus Christ.

Today the Tabernacle provides insight into worship. This insight can help us develop a more intimate relationship with God. This workbook is designed to be used in conjunction with "The Tabernacle" video. It will provide you with a greater understanding of some of the Tabernacle's important elements. You are encouraged to use this workbook as a starting place for additional study.

Each section presents a different portion of the Tabernacle, found in the Key Verse. Within the section are four study levels that encourage you in the following ways:

> The first goal is **UNDERSTANDING** what the purpose and function of each item was intended to be.
>
> Then you can move into **APPLYING** the principle to your spiritual life. You can enhance this part of the study through personal examination and prayer.
>
> Next, you may go **EXPLORING** into further applications and gain a deeper understanding of the spiritual truths of the component.
>
> You will then proceed by **MEDITATING** on a particular aspect of the element.
>
> Finally, the **ADDITIONAL THOUGHTS** section will give you a summary of the overall lesson and engage your mind to deepen your understanding.
>
> Answers for these lessons may be found in the Answer Key beginning on page 43.

As with any study of the scriptures, you will gain more insight by consulting additional resources. Sources you may want to consider include:

> Bible Dictionary
> Concordance
> Bible Handbook / Almanac

For this study I have chosen to use the New International Version of the Bible. If you are using a different translation, you may find your answers vary slightly in wording.
(Be assured though that no difference in meaning or doctrine is intended.)

I encourage you to take time to view the appropriate portion of the video as you study each item. There is no specific amount of time required for this study, however, the amount of time you invest will reveal itself in greater understanding and appreciation of the Tabernacle. This workbook and the knowledge and wisdom you will gain from doing this study is yours to enjoy. I pray that you will reap the benefits.

Shalom,

Ray Neu

Suggested Approaches for Study

1) *Personal Devotions*
   - Do a lesson a day, or a portion of a lesson each day.
   - If you break the lessons down to use one per week, review completed sections as you move forward. This will help you maintain the larger scope of the study.
   - Select a verse to memorize that is meaningful to you.
   - Ask often, what does this mean - to me? -- for me?
   - Develop a journal of practical application steps and spiritual insights as you progress.
   - While at church, reflect on various aspects of the Tabernacle and examine how you participate in similar ways today.

2) *Partnering or Mentor Study*
   - Use the format for Personal Devotions.
   - Meet weekly for review of what you have studied personally.
   - Share or compare notes from each other's study.
   - Set attainable action goals.
   - Share these and hold each other accountable for reaching them.

3) *Sunday School Class - Group Study*
   - Watch the entire video the first week.
   - Move through one lesson each week.
   - Review the video presentation once a month or whenever necessary.
   - Have your class walk through your church and identify items that correspond with the items in the Tabernacle.
   - Role play the functions of the High Priest.
   - Encourage group discussions for the elements of sacrifices and offerings.

4) *Worship*
   - Watch the video.
   - Listen for key points of each element.
   - Note what strikes you about each.
   - Watch the video again.
   - Try watching with the sound turned off, playing praise music while viewing.
   - Allow your thoughts to follow and be led by each element as it appears.
   - Pray whatever you are feeling or thinking throughout.
   - You may want to record some of your thoughts and experiences.

Sanctuary

Key Verse: "Then have them make a **sanctuary** for Me and I will dwell among them."
Exodus 25:8

UNDERSTANDING

The word sanctuary comes from the Hebrew term miqdash (mik-dawsh), meaning consecrated (place).

Psalm 33:13-15, 1 Kings 8:30, Deuteronomy 26:15
God resides in heaven. However, after God rescued the Israelites from Egypt, He decided to live with them as they journeyed to the Promised Land. Since the Israelites were living in tents, God, too, would live in a tent. God gave specific instructions to the Israelites on how to construct His sanctuary on earth.

Exodus 36:3
How did the materials and construction of this sanctuary come together?
_____

Were the materials and labor a burden or a joy? _____

Exodus 36:6-7
Was there any shortage of materials? _____
What did Moses have to do about the offerings? _____

Numbers 3:6-10
Who was allowed in the sanctuary? _____

Numbers 18:7
How did the Israelites view being chosen to serve as a priest?
_____

APPLYING

Leviticus 19:30
What attitudes should you bring into the sanctuary?
_____

I Chronicles 22:19
What were the people supposed to do before they built God's sanctuary?
_____

Psalm 15:1-5
Write in your own words the answer to this question, "Who will be allowed to live with God in His tent?"
_____

Psalm 20:2
What can we expect from the sanctuary? _____
What attributes of God are seen during worship?

    Psalm 63:2 _____

    Psalm 68:35 _____

How should you worship?

    Psalm 150:1 _____

    Psalm 134:2 _____

How should you worship according to Psalm 34:1-3? _____

God's plan has never been to stay inside any tent or even a building. How does *Ezekiel 11:16* reflect this idea? _____

EXPLORING

The Old Testament's view of sanctuary was a foreshadowing of what God intended for future generations. How did the idea of sanctuary change in the New Testament?

Hebrews 9:1 _____

Hebrews 8:2 _____

Hebrews 9:24 _____

What benefits do we attain from the New Testament expression of the sanctuary found in Hebrews 6:19? _____

God dwelt in the Tabernacle. The Word of God is an expression of Him we find in Colossians 3:16. Where does the Word of God find sanctuary? _____

How could we drive God from His sanctuary? (see *Ezekiel 8:6, 23:39 and Zephaniah 3:4*)

_____

MEDITATING

Read *Luke 11:49-52*

What things will God hold *this* generation responsible for?

_____

What things would the Spirit tell you to change?

_____

ADDITIONAL THOUGHTS

The sanctuary of God is a very special place. In this holy and hushed environment we can seek an audience with the one who created us -- the God who has been leading His people since the creation of Adam. God still desires to lead us and to speak to us in a very personal way. This can happen when we come into the sanctuary.

The location of the sanctuary has changed over the millennia that God has been reaching out to man. The physical church building or temple is not nearly as important as the sanctuary we create in our heart. God has chosen to become more personal because He wants a relationship with us.

Think about the element of sanctuary. Challenge your views of where God is and how He works. By limiting your view of God, you limit your ability to understand God. Consequently, if your understanding is limited, then the reality of God in your life will be equally as limited.

Allow God to speak for Himself. Seek God for the sake of who He is.

Dwell

Key Verse: "Then have them make a sanctuary for Me and I will **dwell** among them."
Exodus 25:8

UNDERSTANDING

To dwell means "residing within" and indicates that there is more than one being living in a place at the same time. God had no intention of building a palace for just Himself. Instead, He gave instructions for this temporary home to be built among the Israelites so that He could share it with His people. This home was called the Tabernacle.

Examine Exodus 29:46. What would the people gain from God dwelling among them?
_____

In Deuteronomy 12:11, what other purposes did the Tabernacle serve?
_____

Exodus 33:7 says that there is another purpose for meeting with God. What is it?
_____

APPLYING

Just as there are benefits from living in your own home, there are benefits to "living with" or "dwelling with" God. Search the scriptures below and match them to the benefit.

Scripture	Benefit
Psalm 27:4 ___	**a.** To have the ability/strength to turn from evil and do good.
Psalm 37:27 ___	**b.** To have sickness healed and sins forgiven.
Psalm 61:4 ___	**c.** To "Gaze upon the beauty of the Lord and to seek Him" - to worship Him.
Psalm 69:36 ___	**d.** To "take refuge" - protection, shelter, security.
Psalm 84:4 ___	**e.** To "love His name" - those who love Him gather.
Isaiah 33:24 ___	**f.** To praise Him.

EXPLORING

Evaluate each scripture and discern the point of the verse:

Psalm 5:4 - What cannot dwell where God is? _____

Proverbs 8:12 - What does God dwell in? _____

Isaiah 33:16 - What will God provide for those who dwell with Him? _____

John 5:38 - What warning is included here? _____
_____

MEDITATING

Read Ephesians 3:16-19.

Where is Christ's ultimate dwelling place? _____

How do you establish Christ's place in your heart? _____

ADDITIONAL THOUGHTS

Try to imagine for a moment the place where God lives. Imagine His home in heaven. What does it look like? What does it sound like? Do you see any discord? Is there anything that seems out of place, frantic, or disrupting?

Now, imagine that God comes to live with you. Would you anticipate that some changes would occur in your home? In your life-style? Would there be more peace? Would you reassess your activities, speech, or priorities?

If God came to live with us, I'm sure most of us would completely over-haul our life-style. Yet wouldn't it be beneficial? Couldn't we all gain from more of a godly influence in our homes? I encourage you to spend some time thinking on this proposition. Reflect on what would change if God were to become a houseguest in your family's life. Commit your thoughts to paper and then make them a matter of prayer.

God's dwelling with us is as real as we allow it to be. Our exposure to His holiness should reflect in our daily lives. After all, we shouldn't leave God behind after we leave the church or temple each week.

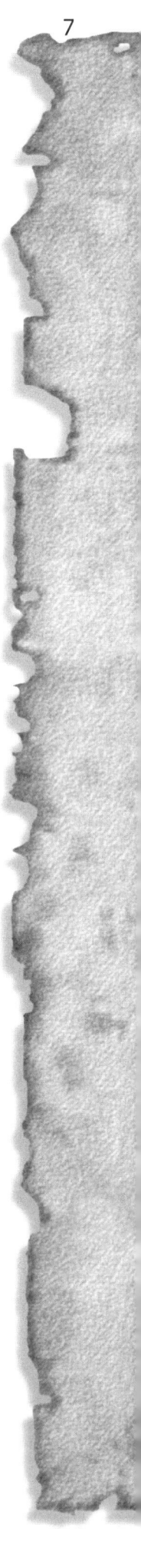

Entrance

*"**For the entrance** to the courtyard, provide a curtain 20 cubits long, of blue, purple and scarlet yarn and finely twisted linen - the work of an embroiderer - with four posts and four bases.   Exodus 27:16*

UNDERSTANDING

The curtain reference in Exodus 27:16 is actually the gate to the Tabernacle courtyard.

Read Exodus 27:9-15

These verses describe the size of the courtyard and the curtains used to mark its boundaries. This brief description implies that the function of the curtains was to separate the consecrated spaces from the people.

In Exodus 40:9-16, all the items and people are listed that Moses was to bless or anoint. Without this consecration you could not approach God's dwelling place.

Check all things that Moses was to anoint:

- ☐ Altar
- ☐ Utensils
- ☐ Animals
- ☐ Basin
- ☐ Stand
- ☐ Aaron
- ☐ Aaron's Sons
- ☐ All Tribes

Read Numbers 18:1-4

Who was to bear the responsibility of offenses against the sanctuary?

_____

Who was to assist them? _____

Where could the Levites go? _____

Where were the forbidden to go? _____

What would happen to them if they went near the altar? _____

Was anyone else allowed near the Tent of Meeting? _____

APPLYING

Why do they need to consecrate themselves? (Leviticus 20:7-8) _____

Who makes them holy? _____

Read Ezekiel 42:20. In this scripture it says that the walls of the Tabernacle were to separate the _____ from the _____.

Ezra 9:1 - Why were the Israelites to separate themselves from the neighboring peoples?

_____

What is God's constant command to us, found in 2 Corinthians 6:17?

_____
_____

EXPLORING

Holiness and separation from uncleanness or sin is an eternal issue with God.

Read 1 Peter 1:16. This verse repeats a statement God made in Leviticus 11:44. What is it? _____

Examine Matthew 25:31-32. What is being separated here? _____

When is this happening? _____

Search Romans 8:35-39. What can separate the believer from God? _____

MEDITATING

Read Ephesians 2:12-13. Does this parallel your personal experience? If not, it easily can. See page 19 for details.

ADDITIONAL THOUGHTS

Even if we don't completely understand it, we all realize that there is something worthy of respect whenever we go to church. We remember when we were younger our mother, father or grandparent would quiet us once we got into the church. As adults we feel a sense of something different when we walk into a church or temple. This is good, because there is something, or rather Someone, different there.

The practice of reverence for God is healthy. In the Old Testament, you could lose your life for not showing proper respect. If this were still happening today, I believe that the problem of hypocrites in the church would completely vanish! Although God is not eager to destroy us, He does want us to approach Him and His house with a certain respect.

Drawing near to God means that we come to Him with purpose and expectation. Merely completing a religious exercise or fulfilling a weekly obligation doesn't keep us in good standing with God. It requires something much more than that. This study is meant to help you discover that.

As you go to your church or temple this week, begin thinking about what you should leave outside. What thoughts, actions, or attitudes would not be conducive to the service? In addition, think about what would be appropriate to take inside with you? What gifts, prayers, and actions would you like to offer to the Lord?

We are not called to be mere spectators. We are invited into a personal, interactive relationship with the living God. Fixing our thoughts in this way will make our weekly church experience entirely worthwhile and very exciting.

Altar

*"Build an **altar** of acacia wood ... it is to be made just as you were shown on the mountain."*
Exodus 27:1,8

UNDERSTANDING
The key to understanding the altar is that it makes holy everything that we offer to God. Many specific offerings and sacrifices were made here. Without this purifying, nothing we could offer to God would be acceptable.

Exodus 29:38-41 - What is the purpose of the altar? _____

Exodus 29:37 - What happens when the offerings touch the altar? _____

APPLYING
How should you approach the altar?

    Psalm 26:6 _____

    Psalm 43:4 _____

What emotions are expressed when approaching the altar?

    Psalm 118:27 _____

    Joel 1:13, 2:17 _____

What should we do before seeking God's forgiveness?

    Matthew 5:23-24 _____

_____

EXPLORING
In God's view, what are the major purposes of the altar?

    Joel 2:17 _____

    Isaiah 56:7 _____

What other major purpose for the altar is listed in Isaiah 6:6-7? _____
_____

Read Malachi 1:7-10, 2:13-15. What displeases God? Check any of the following that apply.

- ☐ defiled food
- ☐ useless fires
- ☐ unacceptable offerings
- ☐ kneeling instead of being prostrate
- ☐ flooding altar with meaningless tears
- ☐ saying that the Lord's table is contemptible
- ☐ extra bushels of grain and wine offerings
- ☐ sacrificing blind, crippled animals
- ☐ unfaithfulness in marriage vow

Read Malachi 1:14. What happens to the one who does not offer God the best?

_____

MEDITATING

Hebrews 13:10-12

What is the altar of verse 10? _____

What do we gain from this special offering (vs. 12)? _____

ADDITIONAL THOUGHTS

Unfortunately, the altar has largely fallen out of use in today's society. The altar is typically seen as a throwback to ancient practices and barbaric customs. Perhaps we don't see the altar for all that it can be because we do not always understand the mystery involved with it. We do not see how a piece of furniture can have any significance in doing business with God. We have become a people who are more apt to want our religion to be private and non-intrusive.

We miss a key element in understanding our relationship with God: He requires that something be given, that we leave some gift to show our heart to Him. The value of the gift is not what is important, since God Himself does not need it. What is significant, however, is that with our gift, God sees that our actions support where our heart is. The widow in the New Testament who gave the incredibly small gift of two mites was cited by Jesus because that was all she had to give. God will take whatever we have to offer and use it in ways that will make it valuable.

An altar offers a beautiful opportunity for people to make peace with God. Here, troubled souls can find solace; wearying burdens can be left behind; and heavy hearts can be lifted. At the altar, people feel a sense of completion. They find a place to confess sins and walk away forgiven. A place where they can cry out for help and leave knowing they have been heard by God. The altar can also be a place of giving thanks for prayers already answered. Here, we can praise God for having given us the strength we desperately needed.

The altar can be a point of contact between a Holy God and a needy people.

In many Christian churches, the altar has been abandoned or replaced with the pulpit. The primary focus of the pulpit is to affirm the preaching of the Word of God. Yet, in the practice of special services and sacraments, we continue to see the need for a centralized point of contact. This is plainly evidenced when individuals present themselves for church memberships, baptism, dedications and even weddings.

Wash

*Key Verse: "Whenever they enter the Tent of Meeting, they shall **wash** with water so that they will not die. Also, when they approach the altar to minister by presenting an offering made to the Lord by fire, they shall **wash** their hands and feet so that they will not die." Exodus 30:20-21*

UNDERSTANDING

Because God is holy, only those who are pure can even approach Him. Since no one is completely pure, the priests would wash with water to symbolically make themselves clean. If anyone regarded this as a mere ritual or took this requirement too lightly, God would apply a stiff penalty for their negligence - death!

Exodus 30:20-21 (Key verse)
   Why were they to wash? _____

Numbers 8:6-7
   What was the purpose of this cleansing? _____

APPLYING

Read the scripture and answer accordingly.

☐ Yes ☐ No	Psalm 51:2,7	Washing cleanses us from sin
☐ Yes ☐ No	Acts 22:16	Baptism is a form of washing
☐ Yes ☐ No	James 4:8	The cleansing James speaks of has a different purpose than in Moses time (compare with Exodus 30:17-21 for further understanding)
☐ Yes ☐ No	Isaiah 1:16-18	God is responsible for washing us
☐ Yes ☐ No	Isaiah 1:17	We should be involved in helping social action
☐ Yes ☐ No	Isaiah 1:18	Once we are washed we still show the stains of sin

EXPLORING

Read John 13:2-15. Note that the physical expressed here is symbolic of the spiritual.

   What did Jesus wash in verse 5? _____

   Why did He do this? (vs. 8) _____

   Why only their feet? (vs. 10) _____

Compare Galatians 6:1-2 to John 13:2-15.

   Who restores the person who sins? _____

Now compare James 5:16, 19-20 to John 13:2-15.

   Who turns a sinner from wrong ways? _____

   How is this accomplished? (James 5:16) _____

MEDITATING

Compare Genesis 2:9 and 3:22-24 with Revelation 22:14.

   What do we regain that we had been banned from? _____

ADDITIONAL THOUGHTS

When children go out to play and it becomes time for lunch, we do not send them to get a bath before they can eat. But at the end of the day, when the results of their energetic play covers their entire bodies, we direct them into the tub!

We are much the same in God's eyes. We do not need complete forgiveness from God every week because we have not completely lost our salvation* and reverted to being pagans. We do, however, need to be forgiven for the sins of the past week. Jesus taught this principle when He washed the disciples feet. At first Peter wanted nothing to do with his master and teacher washing his dirty, stinky feet. But after Jesus explained that He had to do this or Peter could not be a part of Him, then Peter wanted the washing. In fact, he wanted an entire bath - right there on the spot!

When we look at our very faulty righteousness in view of God's perfect righteousness, it is easy to see why we tend to discredit ourselves so much. We simply cannot measure up. However, as God enables us to become stronger in our personal choices, we do sin less. We do not become sinless, but we do sin less because we are actively trying to be more like Jesus.

For example, when you say something to offend your spouse, you do not expect to be divorced from them and hope that they might take you back. Yet, we often see our relationship with God in this way. We think that each sin causes us to be condemned and that because of this, God could not possibly want anything to do with us. Thankfully, God is not like this.

What does God expect from us when we offend Him? He expects the same as your spouse - a sincere, heartfelt apology. This is the function of washing; making sure that our relationship with God is clean and that there is nothing standing in the way of clear communication with Him.

Once we have accomplished this reconciliation with God, we can move on to more intimate communication. But if we neglect to do this, then try as we might, we will just be going through the motions of worship.

Ask yourself often, "Is there anything that I need to clear up between myself and God?" Then fix it. Jesus said if we are at the altar and remember that we have wronged someone, we are to first go and fix it, and then return to worship. You will find it is much easier to worship God when your conscience is clear and clean.

---

* For those who take a hard stance on this issue of salvation, work with me. Remember, this guide is for the entire body. We are seeking to edify.

Sacrifice

Key Verse: I will **sacrifice** fat animals to you and an **offering** of rams.
I will offer bulls and goats. Selah.   Psalm 66:15

UNDERSTANDING

The word sacrifice comes from the Hebrew term zabach (zaw-bahk), to slaughter.
The word offering comes from three Hebrew terms:
- Terumah (teer-oo-maw) - a present
- Minchah (min-khaw) - to apportion, bestow, donate
- Qurban (koor-bawn) - something brought near, a sacrificial present

Read each of the verses and fill in the appropriate letter.

___ Job 1:5	Why did Job offer sacrifices?	a. paying for it
___ Ex. 29:38	How often were offerings to be made?	b. none!
___ 2 Sam. 24:24	What does David insist on doing in regards to the sacrifice?	c. daily
___ I Kings 8:62-63	What is the limit on offerings?	d. to get forgiveness for His children's sins

Select the characteristics or attitude accompanying the offering for each of the following verses:

___ Psalm 27:6	a. prayer
___ Psalm 50:14	b. listen
___ Psalm 54:6	c. shouts of joy/singing
___ Psalm 141:2	d. freewill
___ Ecclesiastes 5:1	e. thanks, fulfilling vows

APPLYING

What is wrong with each of these offerings?

Isaiah 65:3 _____

Amos 4:5 _____

2 Chronicles 28:23 _____

2 Kings 3:27 _____

Read Jonah 2:9 - What conclusion does Jonah come to? _____

Romans 3:25-26 - Who is being sacrificed here and what is accomplished by it?
_____

Romans 8:3-4 - What offering did Jesus become for us?
_____

EXPLORING

What is being compared in I Samuel 15:22? _____

Which of the two is more pleasing to God? _____

Read I Samuel 15:23a.

What is rebellion compared to? _____

What is arrogance compared to? _____

MEDITATING

Mark 12:33

"To love Him with all your heart, with all your understanding, and with all your strength and to love your neighbor as yourself is more important than all the burnt offerings and sacrifices."

ADDITIONAL THOUGHTS

Tithes and offerings are terms that we are familiar with today. However, sacrifice is not a common term. Since money is the commodity of exchange today, it is often the object of our attention, and, too often, our affection. We are familiar with donations, capital campaigns, and fund-raising efforts. There is a seemingly endless parade of clever ways to get us to remove money from our wallets. Now that I have grabbed your attention, and nearly lost it as well, let me move on to say that sacrifice is not primarily about giving money.

Instead of focusing on money, we need to think about the much more important point of sacrifice that we need to give to God and it needs to cost us something. What good is a gift if it costs us nothing?

King David adamantly refused to accept the threshing floor and sacrifices from Araunah, even though these things were willingly offered. King David knew they would not be coming from Araunah's heart. Therein is the key to the matter for us.

Does what we offer to God come from our hearts or from some sense of obligation? The Bible is clear about the fact that God wants us to decide on what we wish to give and then give it cheerfully and not under compulsion. (Yet, sometimes we feel that the pastor is pressuring us into some sense of guilt for not giving enough. Often what we feel is undue compulsion from the pastor, is really the Holy Spirit quietly urging us to be more generous in our giving.)

The Bible is clear that as we give, God gives back to us. (This may not make much sense in a society where we are always anxiously awaiting the next paycheck.) In God's economy though, it is a truth. When we choose to live up to the biblical principles taught throughout the Scriptures, we find they really do work! While it may not make sense to an accountant or other budget minded person, the person of faith will find this very comforting.

If you think this is still just about money, think about the following: What else can be given as an offering to God? Why do we make choices each year during Lent? Why do we try to give more of ourselves during the holiday season? Isn't there a part of you that realizes God is not always interested in just your money? Can you see that there are times when what He most wants is you?

Yes, God desires you. Your time, your interests, your lunch hour. It is God's desire to take anything you are willing to offer Him so that He can show you just how much He can accomplish when you give gladly from your heart. What seems like a small thing to you becomes incredible when the power of God is behind it.

Blood

Key Verse: "Take some of the bull's **blood** and put it on the horns of the altar with your finger and pour the rest of it at the base of the altar."

Exodus 29:12

UNDERSTANDING

The slaughter of this bull was part of the sin offering. In this instance, it was part of the ceremony for the consecration of the priest (Exodus 29). Our purpose here is to understand the role blood played in making sacrifices and offerings.

Exodus 29:14 - What type of offering was this? _____
(Also see Exodus 29:36)

Exodus 29:18 - This ram's sacrifice was a _____ offering that was _____ to the Lord.

Exodus 29:19-21 - The second ram's blood was applied where? _____
_____

Why was this done? _____

After consecration and ordination came the regular daily offerings. According to Exodus 29:38-43, what was offered every morning and evening?

A _____ along with a _____ and _____ offering.

APPLYING

The first seven chapters of Leviticus outline various offerings. You may wish to read these for a fuller understanding, but for our purposes now, look at Leviticus 1:1-5.

What were the physical requirements of the animal to be sacrificed? (v.3)
_____

Where was the animal presented? (v. 3) _____

What action indicated that the animal was for the atonement of the person's sin? (v.4)
_____

According to Hebrews 10:1-4, there is a limitation on what the blood of these animals can accomplish.

In verse 1 it says that the blood cannot make us _____.

In verse 4 it says that the blood of bulls and goats cannot _____ _____ sin.

Hebrews 10:12 and Romans 3:25.

Who is "this priest" mentioned in Hebrews 10:12? _____

What is it that justifies us? (Romans 5:9) _____

Ephesians 1:7
In this verse justification is also called redemption. What else is it called here?
_____

EXPLORING

Hebrews 9:12-14 - Jesus did not approach God with the usual sacrifice. What did He offer instead? (vs. 12) _____

In verse 13, what cleansing does the blood of the bulls and goats offer?
_____

Jesus can cleanse something else. According to verse 14, what does He cleanse?
_____

Hebrews 9:22 states that without blood there is no _____.

Read Hebrews 10:29. Since giving one's life is the ultimate sacrifice, what awaits the person who disregards Jesus' sacrifice of His own body? _____

MEDITATING

Read 1 John 5:6-8. Reflect on how each of these elements appear in the life of Jesus.

The Spirit	a) descending at the Baptism b) being led by the Spirit c) gave up His spirit
Water	a) born of a woman b) baptized c) water from His side at death
Blood	a) born of a woman b) gave His life c) cleanses us from sin - 1 John 1:7

ADDITIONAL THOUGHTS

Now we're getting messy. All this business about the blood seems foreign and unnecessary to some of us, while to others it brings a sense of comfort. How can this be? How can something so...so...well, you know, be comforting? The answer is found in understanding the value and the effectiveness involved with the blood. We may not achieve full appreciation until we come face to face with a time when someone else steps in to save our lives and loses theirs in the process. I use this example because this is really the essence of what we are talking about. In Old Testament practices, an animal's blood was used to achieve atonement for sins. In the New Testament, we are introduced to a radical new idea.

Jesus brought a new system. However, as humans we like to stick with what we know and the old tradition remained the custom for a very long time. Jesus did not completely change the old system, nor do away with it. What Jesus accomplished was actually finishing the old system, perfecting it. He offered the one blood sacrifice that was acceptable not only for those alive then, but for who ever had been alive or ever would be.

The animals sacrificed had to be physically perfect and without blemish. This sacrifice of their blood then achieved a justification inwardly, for the person offering it. Since no person could achieve a state of perfection, animals were substituted to attain this for the person. However, Jesus changed all that. He *did* live the life no one else could ever live. He was perfect.

The Bible clearly tells us that Jesus was tempted in all ways - just like the rest of us. Yet He did not sin. Consequently, He did not even need to ask for forgiveness as we do. Yet He chose to give His life, signified by His blood, so that no other animal need ever die for man's sins. No one would ever have to purchase or raise a healthy animal and then offer that excellent specimen just so they be clean before God.

ADDITIONAL THOUGHTS (continued)

Jesus accomplished this through His death on the cross. Because of His sacrifice, we have a responsibility. 2 Corinthians 5 tells us that we should no longer live for our own desires. Instead, we are to live to fulfill the desires of the One who died for us and then rose again on our behalf. I know of only One person that could be. And I can think of no greater purpose than to do just as we are asked.

Perhaps you have heard it expressed in other cultures, that if someone saves your life, you are indebted to them for the rest of your life. If Jesus has saved your life, how will you repay this debt to Him?

If you are not sure that Jesus has saved your life, this is the time to examine the evidence and see how much He loves you and longs to have a relationship with you.

EXAMINE THE EVIDENCE

Ephesians 2:12-13
> *"Remember that at that time you were separate from Christ, excluded from citizenship in Israel and foreigners to the covenants of the promise, without hope and without God in the world. But now in Christ Jesus, you who were once far away have been brought near through the blood of Christ."*

To fully understand this passage, we need to realize the context of the people the author is writing to. They *were* at one time separated from God, both in terms of religious practice and in belief. But at this point they had gone through a transformation. This change was not just in the form of their religious practice as much as it was in their beliefs and the object of their worship. They had come to the place where they understood that there was more to their beliefs than religious formalism.

They understood that God had prepared a way for them to enter into a personal relationship with Him. This was a huge change from what they were used to. Their former practice of religion did not have a basis of hope without the fulfillment of God's promise, which was accomplished in Jesus Christ. Furthermore, many of them had not even practiced the Jewish faith, so they were completely without any hope.

Perhaps you can relate to the feeling of being without hope. You may not realize that there is even the possibility of a way to find peace. True peace comes from God. He is willing not only to give us peace, but has provided the way for us to finally reach peace. Ephesians 2:14 tells us that Christ is our peace. The next verse tells us ... "*His purpose was to create in Himself one new man...thus making peace."* It is through believing in Jesus Christ that we find peace. Jesus forgives our sins, the wrongful deeds we have done before God, and reconciles us to God so our soul gains peace. This happens when we acknowledge our need for forgiveness and ask Jesus to grant that for us.

ACKNOWLEDGE YOUR NEED

Jesus knows our needs but wants us to come to Him for forgiveness. The process is laid out for us in Romans 10:9-13.

> *"That if you confess with your mouth, "Jesus is Lord," and believe in your heart that God raised him from the dead, you will be saved. For it is with your heart that you believe and are justified, and it is with your mouth that you confess and are saved. As the Scripture says, "Anyone who trusts in him will never be put to shame." For there is no difference between Jew and Gentile - the same Lord is Lord of all and richly blesses all who call on him, for, "Everyone who calls on the name of the Lord will be saved."*

It is your decision. I believe that even now, as you are reading this, you can sense that something is encouraging you to make this decision. You feel a beckoning. Respond to it, do not delay.

2 Corinthians 6:2 compels us forward.

> *"In the time of my favor I heard you, and in the day of salvation I helped you. I tell you, now is the time of God's favor, now is the day of salvation."*

I'm not trying to create fear within you, but I wish to be thorough with you. I must tell you that Jesus had very strong words to say about the decision you are contemplating right now. In Matthew 10:32-33 He lays out this challenge.

> *"Whoever acknowledges me before men, I will also acknowledge him before my Father in heaven. But whoever disowns me before men, I will disown him before my Father in heaven."*

Friend, God is calling you. He shows His great love and desire for us in 2 Peter 3:9.

> *"The Lord is not slow in keeping his promises, as some understand slowness. He is patient with you, not wanting anyone to perish, but everyone to come to repentance."*

If you are unsure how to pray to God, use this sample prayer. The words are not nearly as important as your attitude, since God looks at your heart.

> Dear God, forgive me for my sins. I know that I have done wrong in your eyes. Clean my heart from all that displeases You. I acknowledge my need for Jesus to be my Savior - for my sins as well as the Lord of my life. I trust Him now to show me the right way to live before You.
> In Jesus' name. Amen

You have just made a most wonderful life-changing decision! Record it here as your spiritual birthday.

Today _____ (date), I became a full believer in God's Son, Jesus.

To help you to learn more and to grow as a Christian, we encourage you to visit
www.billygraham.org
for help in taking the additional steps in your relationship with God.

Holy Place

Key Verse: "When Aaron enters the **Holy Place**..."   Exodus 28:29

UNDERSTANDING

The term Holy Place comes from the Hebrew word qodesh, meaning apartness, sacredness, holy. It is important to understand what happened inside the Holy Place and why it happened.

Read each passage listed and check each box that is verified by the verses.

Exodus 28:29-35

a. ☐ Aaron wore a list of his children's names on his chest.
b. ☐ The robe was decorated with blue pomegranates.
c. ☐ Aaron's robe had bells sewn onto it so others could hear him moving around.
d. ☐ Aaron wore a blue robe whenever he entered the Holy Place.
e. ☐ The purpose of the Urim and Thummim was to help make decisions.
f. ☐ The bells were a requirement, the consequence of disobeying was death.

Exodus 40:4-5 - Check the items that were in the Holy Place

☐ Table   ☐ Curtain   ☐ Lampstand
☐ Altar of Incense   ☐ Jars of Oil   ☐ Chair

Exodus 25:29-30 - What belonged on the table?

☐ Plates   ☐ Spices   ☐ Dishes
☐ Meat Offering   ☐ Pitchers   ☐ Bowls
☐ Tablecloth   ☐ Bread of Presence   ☐ Silverware

Read Exodus 27:20-21. When were the lamps to be burned? _____

Read Exodus 30:7-8. When was the incense to be burned? _____

APPLYING

According to Psalm 24:3-4, who can go to the Holy Place?
_____

In Isaiah 63:18 who took over the Holy Place? _____

When a sanctuary or holy place was physically attacked, the battle was obvious. These battles aren't as clear anymore. What are some of the things that happen in today's society that trample the holiness in our sanctuaries? _____
_____

Realize also that everyone may not agree on what is detrimental to our holiness. You should seek direction from the Holy Spirit in these matters and let Him guide your conscience.

EXPLORING

Isaiah 57:15
In what two places does God live?

1. _____   2. _____

What does the first location imply about the second one? For help with this, compare Isaiah 57:15 to I Peter 1:16.

_____

MEDITATING

"He has showed you, O man, what is good. And what does the Lord require of you? To act justly and to love mercy and to walk humbly with your God."   Micah 6:8

Reflect on these qualities before going to church each week. How will this help you prepare for worship?

_____

ADDITIONAL THOUGHTS

Have you ever been around people that seem to know something more about God than you do? Perhaps you have had an elderly grandmother or relative that seemed to shine with something godly. You may have encountered people or even places that you felt were somehow special or set apart. When you were at these places or with these people God seemed to be closer. Such a spot was the Holy Place in the Tabernacle.

The reason that I chose to link certain "godly" people together with certain "holy" places is that in our age, this is how God often reveals Himself. God is not confined to a particular locale. True, we do get a sense that we are in the presence of God when we enter certain temples or churches. But we also get this sense during our personal worship time at home. It is the object of our worship that makes a place or time special. When God acknowledges our worship, we realize we have entered into something special, a relationship with the Creator.

We know that only certain people could go into the holy place within the Tabernacle. This changed with the coming of Jesus. He opened the door for all who would seek God. However, we should still approach God the same way as the priests did. Not that I am speaking of a style of clothing, but an attitude of the heart.

It is with reverence and respect that we come into God's presence. We do not just drop in, make several requests, and leave as if God were our housekeeper. Realize that approaching God is a serious endeavor and should not be taken lightly.

God was disgusted by many of the offerings and sacrifices in the Old Testament because they were just for show. Who may approach God? Only he who has a contrite heart.

Lampstand

*Key Verse: Make a **lampstand** of pure gold..."* Exodus 25:31

UNDERSTANDING

The lampstand served a very important purpose in the plan of the room where it was placed. It held the only light in the room and was the single source of vision for those who came in. It provided the light for the priests to be able to see the Table of Showbread and the Altar of Incense. It also served to show the path to the veil behind which the Ark of the Covenant sat.

Fill in the blanks with words from the list provided.

Word list: incense   morning   table   seven   evening   light

Exodus 25:37 There were _____ lamps on the lampstand. The purpose of the lamps was to provide _____ .

Exodus 27:21 The lamps were used from _____ until _____ .

Exodus 40:4-5 The two items in front of the lamp were the altar of _____ and the _____ .

APPLYING

Psalm 18:28 What does the burning lamp do to the darkness? _____

Psalm 119:105 What does the lamp in this verse do? _____

What is the lamp symbolizing? _____

Proverbs 6:23 What is this lamp symbolizing? _____

What do the commands lead to? _____

Proverbs 20:27 What does the lamp do here? _____

I Samuel 3:1-4 The lamp here is significant to God's _____ to the boy Samuel.

EXPLORING

Read Luke 8:16.

What is the primary purpose of the lamp? _____

Who can see the light? _____

If the lamp were under the bed or people did not come in, what use would the lamp have? _____

Read Luke 11:34-36.

How does your eye serve as a lamp to the body? _____

What does light and darkness symbolize here? _____

How can we determine the amount of light our body is exposed to?

_____

EXPLORING (continued)

Luke 15:8

Why does the woman light the lamp? _____

If we light the lamp of God's word, when we would use it to search for :
    a) lost coins   b) lost dreams   c) lost souls

MEDITATING

Read Revelation 2:4-5

What did we fail to do that could cause our lampstand to be removed?

_____

Remember your zeal when you first became a Christian? Has anything dampened that zeal? Can you change what has occurred? Remember that God can restore anyone.

ADDITIONAL THOUGHTS

The lampstand is a place from which we direct light. We do not plug a light bulb directly into an electrical cord and leave it lying on the floor. We place the light bulb on a lamp and allow the position of the lamp to direct the light where we want it to go. The larger the area we wish to illuminate, the higher we place the bulb on it's respective stand. It may be a lamp in a living room or a spotlight mounted in the ceiling. It may be a lamppost in the front yard or even a lighting tower in a large sports stadium.

The lampstand simply serves a purpose. It helps to dispel darkness. This lampstand is made of gold, which speaks to its value. We will see more about gold in the study about light. Notice that the lampstand does not choose its own location, but faithfully serves until it is moved elsewhere.

The appearance of the lampstand itself may draw further interest. It may even become an object of attraction and attention. This, too, can have purpose in the greater scheme of things. However, notice that if the light were taken away and you could not see the lampstand, what would happen to it's value then? What of its purpose? If there were no light, could you appreciate the beauty of the lampstand?

The lampstand elevates the light. It raises it up so that it brings benefit to all who enter. Christ said, "If I be lifted up, I will draw all men unto Me." The light is lifted up by the humble service of the lampstand. Yet the lampstand is esteemed because of its faithful service. It is only doing what it was designed to do, and in God's eyes, that is enough.

Light

Key Verse: "Then make its seven lamps and set them up on it so that they *light* the space in front of it."   Exodus 25:37

UNDERSTANDING

While the lamp was an important element of the Tabernacle, the light coming from it was even more critical. Light holds great importance in the Bible, specifically in what it symbolizes and what it does for us. Read the following verses and answer the questions.

Psalm 19:8 - What is it that gives light to our eyes? _____

Psalm 78:14 - God used this light to do what? _____

Psalm 89:15 - We should use God's light so we can _____ in His presence.

Job 33:28 - The light here kept Job from going where? _____

Isaiah 42:6 and Luke 2:32 - Who is this light for? _____ and _____

I John 1:5 - God is what? _____

John 8:12 - Jesus is what? _____

APPLYING

Select the correct answer for each question.

    John 8:12 - What kind of life does Jesus give?
        a. to see the future   b. light of life   c. freedom

    John 5:33-35 - Jesus tells us that the light is:
        a. hope   b. truth   c. peace

    Matthew 5:14 - Who is the light here?
        a. Jesus   b. other believers   c. we are - believers

    Psalm 119:130 - What gives the light in this verse?
        a. unfolding God's word   b. submission   c. redemption

    Proverbs 6:20-23 - Verse 20 - Who passes along the commands?
    a. teachers & counselors   b. preachers & deacons   c. fathers & mothers

    Verse 22 - When do they guide us?
        a. when we walk, when we sleep, when we're awake
        b. when we really need help
        c. when we have no options.

    Verse 23 - Light also serves as a form of:
    a. comfort   b. correction/discipline   c. added benefit

EXPLORING

John 9:5 - Who is the light of the world? _____

    When is He the light? _____

In the following passages we will examine what happens after Jesus leaves the world.

Matthew 28:19-20 - Who did He give authority to? _____ and _____

Acts 1:8 - What are we to do? Go and be _____.

EXPLORING (continued)

2 Corinthians 5:14-15 - Who do we live for? _____

Acts 13:47 - Who is this for? _____

Colossians 1:12 - Why are we allowed to be a part of this? _____
_____ .

Acts 26:18 - What is our basic purpose? To open their _____ for _____
and _____ .

MEDITATING

Isaiah 58:8 - What three things happen when your light breaks out?

1. _____
2. _____
3. _____

Isaiah 60:1 - Where does the light come from? _____

Isaiah 60:3 - Who will be attracted to your light? _____

ADDITIONAL THOUGHTS

Gold is attractive. The world holds it in high value because of its rarity and beauty. However, gold does not come out of the ground looking like something you would want to hand around your neck or proudly display on your finger. Instead, it is covered with dirt and sediment and only slightly reflects light. Only after it has been refined are we able to see its beauty. When the dirt has been removed we start to see some of its true color and it begins to take on an attractive appearance. Next, the raw lump of gold ore is exposed to a great light - a fire. This fire purifies the rough condition of the gold. When the fire is hot enough, the gold and dirt melt. It is then that the dirt, now called dross, is skimmed off the surface; leaving behind a purer form of the original gold nugget. This refining process can be repeated numerous times. Each time a more pure form of gold is revealed, thus creating the varying carats of gold we are familiar with.

The fire, and the light associated with it, exposes the impurities found in the gold. The light in the Holy Place acts in much the same way. It shows us our impurities and then helps us divulge them to those around us. At first, the light reveals little that would be attractive, but then as we continue to refine and re-refine ourselves, we can become more pure and more like the image of the One we follow.

The light that we show to others is not actually from us, but is a reflection of the source found within us. We are showing others the results of our continual purification. It is an invitation for them to come closer to the light and find this same purification for themselves.

It is important to point out a couple of truths. First, the gold did not become pure on its own. No gold nugget ever climbed out of the ground and into a fiery pot. We, too, do not seek to expose ourselves to purification, but God calls us to it. Nor do we always appreciate the process as we go through it. However, once it is complete, we rarely disagree that it was completely worthwhile.

Second, since we cannot take sole credit for self-purification, we should remain humble when showing others what is possible in their lives as well. Jeremiah 18:6 points out that just as we are like clay being made into pottery, so it is with the analogy of gold and us. The nugget does not decide what it wants to be. It is up to the discretion of the designer how he will fashion the gold. So it is with us, it is up to God what He desires for us. The fact that we can participate in decisions that affect our lives is a privilege. Ultimately, God decides who He will use and for what purposes.

It is His light that shines within us. It is His will to use us. We can only hope to do our best to reflect His grace.

Bread

*Key Verse: Put the **Bread** of the Presence on this table to be before Me at all times."*
Exodus 25:30

UNDERSTANDING

The Bread of the Presence represented the twelve tribes of Israel and was kept on the Table of Showbread. Bread is a key symbol used throughout the Scriptures.

Read the scriptures below and match the answers to the questions.

____ 1. What type of bread was used? (Exodus 34:18)   a. It is consecrated

____ 2. When was the bread set in place? (Leviticus 24:8)   b. Each Sabbath

____ 3. What did the bread symbolize? (Leviticus 24:8)   c. Because it was consecrated

____ 4. What was done with the bread? (Leviticus 24:9)   d. A lasting covenant

____ 5. Why was the priest hesitant to give David the bread? (I Sam 21:4-6) e. Unleavened

____ 6. What distinction is made of the bread? (Hebrews 9:2) f. Aaron and his sons ate it.

APPLYING

Job 23:12 - What does Job value more than daily bread? _____

Psalm 37:25 - Who receives the promise of having enough bread? _____

Proverbs 30:8 - How much bread does the writer ask for? _____

Isaiah 33:15-16 - List some of the qualities of the man whose bread is supplied for him:

_____   _____

_____   _____

Matthew 4:4 - Besides bread, what is *necessary* for man to live? _____

Matthew 6:11 - How often do we need bread? _____

Is our need for spiritual bread any different? _____

EXPLORING

Read John 6:25-51

In verse 26, why were the people looking for Jesus? _____

In verse 27, what does Jesus tell them to look for instead? _____

What does it say that their forefathers ate in verse 31? _____

In verses 32-35, who does it say gives the true bread from heaven? _____

What is this true bread? _____

EXPLORING (continued)
John 6:50-51 - What lasting benefit comes from eating this bread? _____

Is this   a) physical bread   or   b) spiritual bread

MEDITATING
Read I Corinthians 11:23-26

What does this bread symbolize? _____

What does this "being broken" symbolize? _____

What does the blood symbolize? _____

Slowly digest I Corinthians 11:27-32. Reflect on why so many in our churches are weak and sick. Why is this, according to this passage? _____
What can you do about this? *Will you* do something about this?

ADDITIONAL THOUGHTS
Eating is pleasurable. We do not need to be reminded to eat. In fact, we make detailed plans about what to eat and when and with whom. Much of our energy on a daily basis is given over to the tasks involved with eating. Consider the myriads of restaurants with their special themes, cook books created to appeal to every culinary delight imaginable and even convenience food has it's own rather formidable place in our lives. While it is true that eating is necessary, we have, in many cases, elevated this daily ritual into its own artform.

Why are we not so driven to do the same with reading the Bible? Do we really see it as a casual option tossed out there by a God who merely wrote the book for those who need such a crutch? In doing so, we are treating God's Holy Word as if no recipe for cooking was ever needed. That throwing anything into a pot for any amount of time will always produce the perfectly desired results.

If you have spent any time in the kitchen, you know that this is not so. (Even those who may be able to now cook without recipes have gained that skill as a result of having watched others, combined with many, many hours of their own practice.) To disregard the daily intake that the Bible offers us is to treat the Bible as only raw materials that can be mixed together in any format and will always produce a delectable treat that God Himself would be happy with.

We also know that this is not true. I must challenge each of us to really examine this in terms that are practical enough for us to understand. That is why I have hammered on the food theme for so long. We are so quick to explain our reasons for not reading the Bible everyday. (I'm not disciplined enough, I'm not a reader, I can't understand it, I'm too busy, tired, confused, etc.)

Now try to make these same statements about eating. Do any of these reasons really make sense? Would any of them be an adequate reason not to eat? Are there not many ways to make up for our deficiencies in being able to cook for ourselves? If we cannot cook, we get someone else to do it for us, but we still eat for ourselves. So, if you cannot understand the scriptures, get help. Try another version of the Bible. If you're not a reader, listen to tapes. If you're not disciplined, set an attainable goal and begin to do better.

When tempted by the devil in regards to Jesus' personal hunger after fasting for forty days, He showed us the right relationship even between food and the Bible. His answer was that man does not live by bread alone but by every word that comes from the mouth of God. If this is so and you are not enjoying a regular diet of God's Word, then aren't you sort of starving yourself?

You have my personal promise that as you investigate the Bible and begin to make it a regular part of your spiritual diet, you will find that the Bible is filled with incredible delicacies for you to learn to "feed on" and benefit from. You will also enjoy the verse in Psalm 34:8 that tells us to "taste and see that the Lord is good."

Incense

*"Make an altar of acacia wood for burning **incense**."*   Exodus 30:1

UNDERSTANDING

The incense used in the Tabernacle was very special. It had a certain mixture and very specific purpose. It was only to be used in the offerings to God and any violation of that had dire consequences.

Read the following scriptures and indicate true statements with a T and false statements with an F.

Exodus 30:7-9
- ___ 1. The purpose of this altar was to burn incense.
- ___ 2. Aaron was to burn the incense every morning and evening.
- ___ 3. This altar was also used for candles for extra light.
- ___ 4. This altar was placed in front of the outer entrance.

Exodus 30:34-38
- ___ 1. God describes this incense as most holy.
- ___ 2. The Israelites were allowed to use this incense for themselves.
- ___ 3. Any person who made some for personal use was to give an extra sacrifice.

Leviticus 16:12-13
- ___ The incense created smoke to conceal the Atonement Cover.

Leviticus 24:5-7
- ___ Another purpose of the incense was to flavor the bread.

Note that there is an interesting similarity between the cloud that descended on the mountain when God came to speak to Moses and the cloud that would be created by the incense over the Atonement Cover.

APPLYING

Psalm 141:2 - What is incense symbolic of here? _____

Proverbs 27:9 - If incense is a symbol of prayer, whose heart is joyful? _____

Read these verses and fill in the blank with the appropriate significance of the incense as it represents prayer:

Exodus 30:7-8 - Prayers should be offered every _____ and _____ continually.

Levitcus 24:5-9 - Prayers of _____ for our food.

Revelation 5:8 - The elders are holding golden _____ filled with _____ which is the prayer of the _____ .

Revelation 8:4 - The prayers go before _____ .

EXPLORING

2 Chronicles 26:18 - Who was allowed to burn incense? _____

2 Kings 23:5 - Who did King Josiah order Hilkiah, the priest, to get rid of? _____

EXPLORING (continued)

What sin did these priests commit? _____

If this incense was the same mixture as detailed in Exodus 30:34-38, then what should happen to the priests? _____

Jeremiah 1:6 and 7:9
What will God do because the people burned incense to other gods? _____

Jeremiah 11:12
Considering incense as a symbol of prayer, what effect does the citizens crying out to other gods produce? _____

MEDITATING

Read and meditate on Malachi 1:11
  Where will incense/prayers be offered? _____

  Where will God's name be great? _____

Reflect on this verse. Imagine faces of people all around the world, every nationality you can think of, bowing in prayer to God.

ADDITIONAL THOUGHTS

As incense symbolizes prayer we can see some correlations. Prayer is not to be used casually. It is not to be used irreverently. (It is not a magic potion that you can use to get anything you want. It is not to be offered to any other person or idol or so called deity.) It is reserved for God alone. Prayer is a very special element in our relationship with God.

In the Tabernacle, only the priests could burn the incense. Today, we have some who still hold this narrow application of prayer, that only certain individuals duly recognized by the church may pray to God. That simply is not so. I Timothy 2:8 tells us what God's desires for prayer are. "I want men everywhere to lift up holy hands in prayer, without anger or disputing." That includes you and I. The focus and direction of our prayers is the same as the incense in the Tabernacle. Just as the incense ascended to God's throne, so do our prayers.

Our prayers should reflect our hearts. If we are happy, sad, disturbed, confused, needing comfort, or anything else in the realm of human emotion, we should express that to God. You may think it odd that I say this, but this is exactly what David did. The Psalms are the expressions of his heart, filled with either wonder or fear, being poured out to God. God already knows what we are dealing with but He will not break into our lives without an invitation. Thus, we pray.

What we cannot do is to offer these prayers to anyone except God. To pray to other people in this manner, seeking their favor, or to pray to other gods, is completely unacceptable. God will not allow it nor will He hear your prayers when they are not directed solely to Him. He also will not accept prayers that are not offered from a pure heart. If your prayers do not seem to be "reaching" God, then examine what may be wrong on your end. Is there a sin to confess? Is there something that God has asked you to do that you are not doing? Is there something in the way that you are praying that shows that you are not expecting an answer or that you will only accept a certain answer?

God is not to be manipulated. He is always willing to hear our prayers. But we must remember that our prayers are requests, not demands that we make on God. We should also remind ourselves that simply because we make the request does not mean that we will always get exactly what we want, in the way that we want it, at the time we want it. Sound unfair? It is not. We do the same with our children and we should realize that this describes our relationship with God. We are His children and He will answer us in the way that will serve us the best while remaining consistent to His will.

Curtain

Key Verse: *Make a **curtain** of blue, purple, and scarlet yarn and finely twisted linen, with cherubim worked into it by a skilled craftsman."* Exodus 26:31

UNDERSTANDING

This curtain, or veil, was special. It separated the Holy Place, the first room of the Tent of Meeting, from the Most Holy Place. It was similar in color to the curtains at the entrance to the Tent of Meeting and the courtyard, but was distinguished by the cherubim worked into its design. It was also unique in that it was only opened once a year.

Leviticus 16:2 - What was the result of passing through this curtain uninvited? _____

Why? _____

Exodus 33:20 - Why would this cause death? _____

Leviticus 16:11-17 - Why would Aaron take incense behind the curtain?
_____

What was the primary purpose for Aaron's being here? _____

Who else was to assist Aaron? _____

APPLYING

The passages above suggest the very serious purpose of the veil. In this we see a stark illustration that God's holiness is more important than human life. Now in the passages below, select the correct answer to complete the sentence.

    Numbers 4:4-6, 9 - The curtain covered the ark _____
        a) always
        b) during the evenings
        c) when traveling

    The hides of _____ were one of the protective coverings when traveling.
        a) camels
        b) sea cows
        c) sheep

    While traveling, the lampstand was _____
        a) carried high for all to see the light was still leading them
        b) wrapped carefully to avoid scratching
        c) covered to avoid being seen by anyone.

    What does this say about the average person's ability to approach God's presence?
    _____

    Numbers 4:17-20 - Workers were selected from _____
        a) various tribes of the Israelites
        b) only the Kohathites
        c) anyone who wanted to volunteer

    The workers could see the Ark _____
        a) when dismantling the Tabernacle
        b) when setting up the Tabernacle
        c) never

APPLYING (continued)
You would know if anyone sneaked a peek at the ark because _____
- a) they would die!
- b) they would contact leprosy
- c) God would tell Moses

EXPLORING

The curtain, or veil, remained an essential piece in worship until the time of Christ.

Matthew 27:50-51
What happened to the curtain at the time of Christ's crucifixion?
_____

Since a man could not reach the top of the curtain to tear it, how did this happen?
_____

MEDITATING

Examine the purpose of the veil in 2 Corinthians 4:3-4.

What does it cover? _____

Who is it that cannot see? _____

Who is responsible for using the veil to blind them? _____

John 12:31 and John 14:30
Who is this? _____

After considering these verses, ask the Holy Spirit to guide your prayers.

ADDITIONAL THOUGHTS

I am very glad that this veil has been removed. I fully understand that God is so holy that we cannot approach Him. Our sinfulness cannot co-exist in the same place as God's holiness.

For the curious, the thought of a place we are not supposed to see is almost tantamount to disaster, since we want to see what we are not supposed to. This could have had disastrous results in Israel's time. Today, the same type of "risking the forbidden" still leads many into trouble. We are people that do not like boundaries. Yet, God has constructed them for our benefit.

The boundary signified by the veil was kept in place until Christ's death. When Jesus was on the cross and cried out as He gave up His Spirit, the veil in the Temple was torn in two from top to bottom. God was signifying that He had just instituted a new policy. He would no longer remove himself from the reach of the average man or woman. God was open and accessible to all who would come.

Think about how this affects your relationship with God. He is waiting for each of us to come into His presence, to have an audience of one with Him. We do not need anyone else to go before us or represent us. Although, we will see more later about how Christ does represent us before God.

Imagine that you are sitting alone with God. You have His undivided attention. What would you talk about? What have you always wanted to say to Him? What would He say to you? Now, don't just imagine it - do it, because it is happening right now.

Most Holy Place

Key Verse: Hang the curtain from clasps and place the ark of the Testimony behind the curtain. The curtain will separate the Holy Place from the **Most Holy Place.**"

Exodus 26:33

UNDERSTANDING

We have all seen images of a guru or holy man sitting atop a mountain somewhere seeking enlightenment. The idea is that in order to find God, we need to achieve some higher level of existence. Throughout the ages many have sought this elusive "higher spirituality" through any number of means, including meditation, fasting, self-humiliation, or even drugs. As you can imagine, abuses do not mean that we will find God. However, to not completely disparage the attempts of those who sense something in the great beyond, we need to examine this a bit further.

Exodus 26:34 - What single item was placed inside the Most Holy Place? _____

Leviticus 16:2 - Was the Most Holy Place always accessible? _____

    Why? _____

Leviticus 16:16-17 - Why did Aaron, as High Priest, go into the Most Holy Place?
_____

What does verse 16 tell us about where the Tent of Meeting was?
_____

Was the Most Holy Place affected by sin (verse 17)? _____

Was it capable of being cleansed? _____

APPLYING

In Leviticus 16:29-34 it speaks of the Day of Atonement, when all people are cleansed from their sins. Read the scriptures below and match the answers to the questions.

____ 1. How often did the Day of Atonement take place (Lev. 16:34)   a. Through His blood/death

____ 2. Where was the Most Holy Place? (Hebrews 9:3)   b. Holy Spirit

____ 3. What specific sins of the people were atoned for? (Hebrews 9:7)   c. Once a year

____ 4. What is the primary purpose of these washings? (Hebrews 9:10)   d. Cleanses conscience and allows us to serve God

____ 5. What is it that gifts and sacrifices cannot do? (Hebrews 9:9)   e. Behind the second curtain

____ 6. Who teaches us the way into the Most Holy Place now? (Hebrews 9:8)   f. Clear the conscience of the worshipper

____ 7. How did Christ enter the Most Holy Place? (Hebrews 9:11-12)   g. External regulations

____ 8. What two things does this accomplish? (Hebrews 9:14)   h. Sins committed in ignorance (i.e. You are to take care of the ones you know about!)

EXPLORING
Read Romans 3:22-26 and answer the questions below.

1) Who is the sacrifice for atonement? _____

2) What does this accomplish? _____

3) How do we participate in this justification? _____

4) Why do we need this? _____

MEDITATING
Hebrews 10:19-20

What has Jesus' death done for us in regards to the Most Holy Place?
_____

How should we approach the Most Holy Place? _____

If you were to enter the Most Holy Place right now and wait for God to speak to you, what do you think He might talk to you about?

ADDITIONAL THOUGHTS

The Most Holy Place, or Holy of Holies, was an incredibly significant place. The mystery that shrouds this room is intense. Once a year, the High Priest would prepare himself for a face to face meeting with God. Tradition tells us that the other priests would keep him up the night before he was to enter by reading Scripture to him. He had to make certain that there was no sin being harbored in his life. This was not the same as saying to your friends, "No, really. I'm okay." To enter into God's presence with sin in his life would mean his instantaneous death. Some have said that they would also tie a rope around his ankle in case of the unthinkable so they could pull him out without entering into this awe and fear-inspiring place.

Once inside, this man, who would be held in immense respect from the rest of the Israelites would actually hear from God. Imagine! God would speak to this man! There is something tantalizing about imagining this. There is something inviting to us as well. We may wish we could have been the one to enter, to hear the voice of God speaking to us. Then, to be the only one who could share that with the rest of our community. There is something other-worldly about this encounter.

Many of us want, no, *need* to know that God is real. We need to know that the God of the universe who holds all of creation in His hands, is still personal enough to speak to us individually. We reason that if He is personal enough to speak directly to us, then He can hear us as well. Since He can hear us, then our prayers are actually going somewhere. They have purpose. Praying with purpose and knowing God is listening lets us achieve a deeper level of intimacy with Him.

As an analogy, a relationship with God can be seen in the different types of relationships we have with people. We have acquaintances first, then friends, followed by close friends and finally intimate relationships. The latter are where we share our most treasured thoughts and fears. These are the people who know everything about us. We entrust them with our deepest thoughts and fears.

God wants us to communicate with Him on such an intimate level. We should hold back nothing and give Him everything. We should know that we can tell Him everything, regardless of how despicable or silly it may seem. It is all equally important to Him. It is knowing that He seeks only what is absolutely best for us. So we will listen attentively and obey wholeheartedly. This is the essence of entering into the Most Holy Place.

Priests

Key Verse: *Have Aaron your brother brought to you from among the Israelites, along with his sons Nadab and Abihu, Eleazar and Ithamar, so they may serve Me as **priests**."*

Exodus 28:1

UNDERSTANDING

Read Exodus 28:1-5

Who was chosen by God to serve as priests? _____

Why were they given special clothes to wear? _____

Who would make these garments? _____

Where did they get this special skill? _____

Circle all the garments that were made.

    breastpiece   earrings   sandals

    ephod   woven tunic   turban

    robe   leather belt   sash

Read Exodus 28:40-43

What garments were specifically made for Aaron's sons? (verse 40)

_____   _____   _____

What other garment were Aaron and his sons to wear? _____

You will notice that there is a difference in the garments in these two lists. Read Leviticus 21:10 to discover what the distinction is.

Who were the first garments made for? _____

Leviticus 16:15-17 - What special purpose did the High Priest perform once a year?
_____

Hebrews 5:1 - What is the purpose of the High Priest?
_____

APPLYING

Hebrews 5:4 - Can one choose to become a High Priest? _____

Hebrews 5:5-6 - Who became a High Priest? _____

Hebrews 7:16 - What was the basis for Jesus becoming a High Priest? _____

Hebrews 7:18 - The former regulation that the High Priest kept was _____

Hebrews 7:19 - We draw near to God now through a _____

EXPLORING

Read Hebrews 7:23-28 and answer the questions to the corresponding verses.

What is unique about Jesus' length of service? (vs. 23-24) _____

Why does Jesus live? (v. 25) _____

What does this mean? _____

What does this intercessory prayer accomplish? (v. 25) _____
_____

What are Jesus' qualifications for priest? (v. 26) _____
_____

What else distinguishes Jesus from other priests? (v. 27) _____
_____

MEDITATING

Think about the following scriptures:

> Hebrews 8:1-2 - "The point of what we are saying is this: We do have such a high priest, who sat down at the right hand of the throne of the Majesty in heaven, and who serves in the sanctuary, the true tabernacle set up by the Lord, not by man."

Do you actively recognize Jesus as the High Priest in your life?

> Hebrews 4:14 - "Therefore, since we have such a great high priest who has gone through the heavens, Jesus the Son of God, let us hold firmly to the faith we profess."

ADDITIONAL THOUGHTS

The role of the High Priest was intense. The weight of the spiritual and many times, physical well-being of an entire nation rested on him. It was his responsibility to guide them in their actions toward the God that they feared. He would also approach that same God once a year in a direct encounter that no one else desired to do. When God invited the people to come up to meet with Him on the mountain, the people responded in fear. They saw the clouds and heard the thunder that shook the entire mountain and told Moses to go talk to God himself, but to not let God talk to them lest they should die.

God conceded to their fear in the position of the High Priest. Instead of meeting individually and personally with His children, God would speak to them through a spokesperson. That same person would convey the people's thoughts back to God. While not representing God's personal choice, this system was used for hundreds of years. The problem, as with any system, was that it could be and eventually was abused.

Jesus became the final High Priest. His function was to talk to the people on behalf of God the Father. To establish a new system that was being inaugurated through Him. Jesus' purpose was to successfully secure the communication between God and the common people. He did this through His death on the cross. We will talk more about what this accomplished in the next lesson, but for the purposes of this lesson, realize that it opened a direct line of communication between each believer and God Himself. There was no longer a reason for any intermediary.

(continued on next page)

ADDITIONAL THOUGHTS (continued)

The Bible tells us that we have been granted direct personal access to God. We have also become united in our efforts in a new way that makes us all priests! I Peter 2:9 says "But you are a chosen people, a royal priesthood, a holy nation, a people belonging to God, that you may declare the praises of him who called you out of darkness into his wonderful light." Now, before you go out and get a robe and start burning incense, some time should be given to what that means in the new system. We do not have the time or space here to adequately investigate this new position. Let me briefly explain that this has to do with us carrying out the works that Jesus modeled for us while He was here. Jesus Himself said that the things He did, we would do also, and even greater things because He was going to the Father. In a simple sense, we are now His hands. We are the instruments through which the Father's will is accomplished.

Some things to ponder. Search for an answer to these questions.

The High Priest would go into the Holy of Holies and hear from God Himself. He would then share this with the people.

1) How does this happen today, as all believers are to be priests? Search 2 Peter 1:21 and I Peter 1:12.

   _____

   _____

2) What does God say to us that we are to share with others? Look at 2 Timothy 3:16-17.

   _____

   _____

3) How does He send specific messages that may not be found elsewhere? Read I Corinthians 12:8.

   _____

   _____

Are you listening?

_____

Are you serving as a priest?

_____

Covenant

*Key Verse: Then he took the Book of the **Covenant** and read it to the people. They responded, "We will do everything the Lord has said; we will obey."*
Exodus 24:7

UNDERSTANDING

Inside the Holy of Holies was one piece of furniture, the Ark of the Covenant. We will focus here on the covenant, since the ark, while revered and admired throughout the ages, was not meant to draw great attention. It is merely a house for the important document inside - the covenant between God and man.

A covenant is typically used to describe a contract between two parties, with each contributor to hold up his side of the agreement. However, in the case of the covenant God made with mankind, it has nothing to do with man's ability to verify his side. God is the guarantor and upholds the entire covenant Himself.

Exodus 34:28 - What is referred to as the Covenant in this passage? _____

Exodus 24:3-8 - What is the covenant called here? _____

How were the people responsive to the Covenant? _____

Perhaps the best known Covenant is called the Abrahamic Covenant found in Genesis 12:1-3. Read this passage and answer the following:

God was going to develop Abraham into a _____.

How would God treat those who dealt with Abraham? _____

Who would be affected by this Covenant with Abraham? _____

APPLYING

Examine Deuteronomy 29:1, 9-15, then answer the following:

Who is the covenant between? (v. 1) _____

What are the people to do? (v. 9) _____

What did God seal the covenant with? (v. 12) _____

What did God promise to do? (v. 13) _____

Who else is this covenant for? (vs. 14-15) _____

What would break this covenant? (v. 9) _____

Deuteronomy 29:19 - How can a person think they are safe under the covenant when they really are not? _____

Deuteronomy 29:24-25 - When people ask why God has allowed bad things to happen, what is the explanation? _____

Hosea 6:7 - How have these people broken the covenant with God? _____
_____

Malachi 2:8-10 - What else can we do that breaks the covenant? _____
_____

EXPLORING

Read Matthew 26:28 - Who confirmed the covenant and how did he do it?
_____

Acts 3:25 - Does the covenant with Abraham extend to us today? _____

Galatians 3:17 - What does the Law do for the covenant? _____

MEDITATING

Hebrews 8:6-10
    Why is Jesus' covenant better? _____

    What will God do with this new covenant? _____

Matthew 26:28
    What is it that makes Jesus' covenant better? _____
    _____

Hebrews 10:29-31
    What awaits the person who takes the covenant too lightly and does not obey it?
    _____

ADDITIONAL THOUGHTS

God's covenant with man is something that we cannot fully appreciate until we realize how far short we fall from even coming close to meeting *any* of God's standards. If it were not for His incredible grace, we could not ever hope to apply His promises to our lives and receive any of His blessings. Thankfully, God is true to His Word and His character. He is loving and gracious, slow to anger and abounding in grace.

Even in modern times, the strength of a contract is only as good as the one guaranteeing it. Fortunately, the Covenant of God with man is backed by God Himself. The Scriptures also tell us that no covenant is confirmed without blood and we see once again God's provision for this in the death He allowed His Son Jesus to endure. Everything pertaining to the success of this covenant came from God.

The only thing man had to do at all was to obey His commands. It should be an easy thing. Especially for those of us who have lived since the time that Jesus walked the earth. All those who lived before Jesus had to believe and have a certain hope that God would indeed confirm His promise with something more than the blood of bulls and goats. All those who have lived since that time can see what God did to confirm His promises. We should actually have an easier time believing and therefore hold to our faith much more strongly. However, one issue is the same for everyone that has ever lived.

        Will we believe that God's Word is true?

        Will we believe what Jesus said and did while here on earth?

        Will we believe that it is something more than just religious stories?

The promise is good.

The One who promised is good.

The evidence and the list of those who have believed before us is good.

Each of us should ask - what will I do with it?

Presence

Key Verse: "The Lord replied, 'My **Presence** will go with you, and I will give you rest'."
Exodus 33:14

UNDERSTANDING

The word presence comes from the Hebrew word paneh (paw-neh), meaning face. The implication of its root word is to turn to face. We need to see this as we say, in common terms, of "being in someone's face"!

It is an interesting study to trace God's presence through the Bible. You may immediately think, 'Well, He's everywhere, all the time'. That assumption, while factual from the stand point of an Omnipresent God, does not do justice to the point of just what presence means. It carries with it the connotation of a face to face experience, actually being in the presence of someone. Let's examine some of the times and ways God shows up in Scripture.

Adam - In the Garden of Eden, Adam and Eve are treated to knowing God in a way that no one else ever gets to. After sin makes *its presence* known, however, they are also the first to experience a most horrendous separation from God.

Read the following passages and check all that apply:

Genesis 2:15-25, 3:8. In addition to working in God's own garden, what special privileges did Adam and Eve have with God.
___ Talk with Him   ___ Dine with Him   ___ See Him
    ___ Walk with Him   ___ Pray with Him   ___ Fear Him

Genesis 3:6-7, 10-11, 23-24. What caused Adam and Eve's relationship with God to change?
___ Listening to the serpent   ___ Wanting to be more than they were
    ___ Eating the fruit   ___ Getting angry at God   ___ Being lazy

What was the result of their disobedience?

___ Having to leave the garden   ___ Wearing clothes   ___ Pain in childbirth
___ Understanding shame & guilt   ___ Having to work without enjoyment
___ Being separated from God   ___ Passing sin to their children

Genesis 4:8-16 True/False
   T or F Cain had to leave God's presence because of a bad offering.
   T or F God did not care what happened to Cain anymore.
   T or F Cain was happy to be free from an oppressive God.
   T or F Cain still enjoyed the presence of God.

Deuteronomy 4:37-39 - What brought the Israelites out of Egypt? _____

   What else would God do for them? _____

   Who else does it say could do this? _____

Exodus 19:16-25 - Where was Moses to meet with God? _____

   Who else was invited to go with him? _____

   Were the priests to go with him? _____

APPLYING

Read Exodus 33:7-17

When Moses went to the tent to meet with God, who went with him? _____

Where were the people? _____

When did they come near to worship? _____

How does this compare to what is said of the priests in the Exodus 19 passage?
_____

What correlation do you see to modern day church services? _____
_____

What did God say He would do for the people? _____

What stipulation did Moses put on God's Presence? _____
_____

Exodus 34:29-35 tells us about Moses use of a veil after speaking to the Lord God because of the glory of God shining from his face. When he went back to speak to God he would remove it.

What purpose does a veil over the face serve? _____

What does that visual picture of the removed veil say to you in terms of our communication with God? _____
_____

EXPLORING

Exodus 25:30 - What was placed on the table? _____

We know from earlier studies that this bread was an offering to God. It was replaced fresh every week and was then eaten by the priests. This provision that was offered to God and then returned to the priests symbolizes God's provision and is symbolic of His Presence

What, then are the priests serving before the people? _____

As frankincense was an aromatic spice, what would that indicate about the nature of the relationship between God and man, through the priests?
_____

Who was/is in God's presence in heaven?

In Job 1:12 _____

In Isaiah 63:9 _____

MEDITATING

Read Hebrews 9:24. Why is Jesus in heaven? _____

Imagine what Jesus may be saying to God on your behalf right now. What would you want Him to say for you? Why not tell God yourself - right now!

ADDITIONAL THOUGHTS

One can quickly see that the Presence of God is many things to many people at many different times. We have touched ever so briefly on several aspects of what it is to be in God's presence, but cannot in this single lesson give it the proper attention needed. An entire shelf of books would not get us much further than if we devoted a year to the topic. Indeed, this is to be the pursuit of one's entire life. That being said, let me attempt to give you a very brief brush stroke of some of my observations as to how God has revealed His Presence throughout the ages spanned by the Scriptures.

God established a relationship with the very first man He made. His desire and enjoyment of this was seen in the leisurely walks in the garden talking with Adam. The breakdown of this relationship was painful to God and difficult for man to overcome since he was the offending party. The offenders always struggle to humble themselves enough to repair the breach. We see this throughout all of the rest of Biblical history.

In Moses' time, he crossed the breach. He made it to the place where no one else had gone. He nearly reached the same level of personal interaction that Adam enjoyed. Moses talked to God and God talked to him as a man would speak - face to face. (Read that sentence again!) We cannot understate the significance of this truth. It is tremendous! What had been lost was once again found! Moses, because of this very special relationship, became a symbol of Christ in the Old Testament. He was also the hope that men could once again maintain a personal relationship with their Creator.

However, for most of mankind, that proves to be too much to handle. God's requirements of holiness constantly wage war against the personal desires to indulge in any and every form of wickedness. Yet, not everyone would crumble in these battles. I believe we can see the evidence of individuals striving to find God's presence in the midst of every generation.

In Moses time, the priests served to present the presence of God to the people. They were intermediaries between a righteous God and a sinful people. The functions of the priests were to help close the gap. A problem developed when the priests themselves became unrighteous.

God used judges to free Israel. During the time of each judge's life, Israel would not only enjoy freedom from the tyranny of other nations, but they had a time of peace with God. Left to their own devices after each righteous judge would die though, they quickly returned to their wicked ways. In wanting the seeming pleasures of other nations, they too wanted a King. God grudgingly granted this.

The kings served God then as primary intermediaries but were very often too polluted with sin to be of service. God supplied an additional voice for Himself to be heard as He established the prophets.

The prophets served as God's mouthpiece and while not being the ideal situation for developing two way communication, at least the people could hear from God. Once the prophets themselves became unreliable and the people completely given over to pursuing sin, God had no other choice. He became silent.

The relationship was severed. His people were so far from where they needed to be and He was so weary of hearing their complaining that He did the only other thing He could. He stopped speaking and left us alone for 400 years.

The next attempt God made to re-establish the relationship with man was His most aggressive attempt yet. He removed every potential barrier and spared no expense. He sent a special prophet, who could not be corrupted, to announce the introduction of His own Son - Jesus.

(continued on next page)

ADDITIONAL THOUGHTS (continued)

Every system God had instituted in the past had become corrupted and had to be released. Even though men kept the traditions alive through their own efforts, God had stopped listening. Jesus was different. He could not be corrupted. His obedience was perfect to all of God's commands and even His day to day leading. This re-established the communion between God and man and opened the door for each of us to realize our own personal relationship with our Creator. The final act of Jesus was to make this accessible for all of us through sending the Holy Spirit who guides us into this truth.

King David had touched on the beauty of being in God's presence. He treasured it until he too corrupted the sanctity of their relationship. Once it was gone, he felt the incredibly intense pain of that separation. In despair, he cried out to God in Psalm 51:11, "Do not cast me from your presence or take your Holy Spirit from me."

God's eternal desire for men and women to come to Him has been reaffirmed throughout the ages. Regardless of what the generation or even an entire culture may have been engaged in, if there were just one person who desired to be in God's presence, God would meet him where he was and teach him to know his Creator personally. This is our encouragement today as well. God's word still speaks very clearly that His desire for a relationship has not changed since He created Adam.

He still calls out to say, "Whoever will call on the name of the Lord…"

Quick Reference Guide

The guide on the following page can be used to quickly review the entire study. It can also serve as a guide for your personal worship time. Use each keyword to think and pray your way through a virtual walk-through of the tabernacle. Your personal goals may vary, but keep in mind that the overall sense should be that each step leads you closer to God.

As you encounter each item, reflect on its purpose and pray along the guidelines suggested. Allow the Holy Spirit to guide your time so that you are not rushed. Tarry whenever and for as long as you care to.

It is strongly recommended that you complete the entire workbook and review the author's comments at the end of each study before beginning this worship exercise. Doing so will greatly enhance your understanding and appreciation as you seek an audience in God's presence.

As the High Priest would diligently prepare for his once a year visit, I encourage you to be equally as diligent in listening to the quiet whisper in your spirit.

Quick Reference Guide

KEYWORD	SYMBOLIZES	APPLICATION	PRAYER POINT
Sanctuary	Safe & sacred place	Know that you are safe when you're with God	"Thank You, God, for being my shelter and show me how to be pure before you."
Dwell	Live with, share space	Know that He makes it sacred or holy	"Thank You, God, that of all the places You could live, You choose to live in me."
Entrance	The way in, gate, door	Realize that God is approachable	"Thank You, God, that You do not shut Yourself off as a mystery no one can solve."
Altar	Place of sacrificial giving	Realize that our relationship with God will cost us something	"Lord, help me give and serve sacrificially, not just from convenience."
Wash	Cleanness, purity	Know that it is God's desire for us to be clean in His eyes	"Father, thank You, for choosing to see me as a clean and acceptable child of God."
Sacrifice / Offering	Act of sacrificial giving	Consider your motives for giving to or serving God	"Lord, purify my motives so I will give and serve wholeheartedly."
Blood	Attonement, forgiveness	Realize and appreciate that each blood sacrifice means that a living being gave up its life	"Father, thank You for allowing Your Son to give such a great gift for me."
Holy Place	Set apart, distinctly pure	Realize that the closer you draw to God the more purity is demanded	"Holy Lord, search my heart and purify me. Keep me from giving in to temptation."
Lampstand	The place our light shines	Realize our responsibility as bearers of the light and witnesses	"Show me, God, how to help others to see You in my life."
Light	The Truth, Jesus	Actively show how the Truth of Jesus affects our lives	"Lord, help me live outwardly the way Your truth teaches us inwardly."
Bread	God's provision	Acknowledge that everything you have comes from God	"Father, thank You, for being so generous, gracious and giving to me and my family."
Incense	Prayer	Realize the need for continually bringing everything to God in prayer	"Lord, teach me to pray, to speak, and to listen."
Veil/Curtain	Secret Place of God	Realize that you can always go farther and deeper in your relationship with God	"Holy God, let me not esteem you lightly. Cause me to hunger for a deeper and more mature spiritual fruit in my life."
Most Holy Place	Intimacy with God	Realize that God wishes to speak to me personally	"Sovereign Lord, speak now, for your servant is listening."
High Priest	Jesus	Acknowledge Jesus as God's chosen High Priest who intercedes for me	"Thank You, Father, for providing me with Your Son, who not only brings me to You, but also pleads for me."
Covenant	God's Promise	Realize that once God has spoken it, I need only to believe it.	"Lord, help me find and believe the promises in Your Word that are for me."
Presence	Being with God	Realize that as much as we know of God, it is still incomplete until I am with God in heaven	"Eternal Father, give me the hunger to long for the things of heaven."

Answer Key

SANCTUARY
- *Understanding*
  - Exodus 36:3 - Received offerings
    - Joy
  - Exodus 36:6 - No
    - Restrain them!
  - Numbers 3:6-10 - Aaron and His sons and the Levites
  - Numbers 18:7 - As a gift
- *Applying*
  - Leviticus 19:30 - Reverence and obedience
  - I Chronicles 22:19 - Devote their hearts and souls to seeking the Lord
  - Psalm 15:1-5 - An upright and just man who exhibits Godly characteristics in his life
  - Psalm 20:2 - Help
  - Psalm 63:2 - Power and glory
  - Psalm 68:35 - Awesome God - He gives power and strength
  - Psalm 150:1 - Praise
  - Psalm 134:2 - Lift up your hands
  - Psalm 34:1-3 - With our lips - sing
  - Ezekiel 11:16 - God has been a sanctuary for them wherever they went
- *Exploring*
  - Hebrews 9:1 - Earthly - with regulations
  - Hebrews 8:2 - A sanctuary set up by the Lord, not with human hands
  - Hebrews 9:24 - Heaven
  - Hebrews 6:19 - Hope as an anchor for the soul - it is firm, secure
  - Colossians 3:16 - In our hearts
  - Ezekiel 8:6, 23:39, and Zephaniah 3:4 - Detestable things, sacrifice children to idols, desecrated the sanctuary, do violence to the law
- *Meditating*
  - Luke 11:49-52 - The blood of all the prophets that has been shed from the beginning of time

DWELL
- *Understanding*
  - Exodus 29:46 - They will know I am the Lord their God
  - Deuteronomy 12:11 - As a place to bring burnt offerings and sacrifices, tithes, special gifts, vows
  - Exodus 33:7 - Seeking or inquiring the Lord (prayer)
- *Applying*
  - Psalm 27:4   C
  - Psalm 37:27 A
  - Psalm 61:4   D
  - Psalm 69:36 E
  - Psalm 84:4   F
  - Isaiah 33:24 B
- *Exploring*
  - Psalm 5:4 - Evil, wickedness
  - Proverbs 8:12 - Prudence, knowledge, discretion
  - Isaiah 33:16 - Bread, water (bread represents the Word of God, water represents the Spirit
  - John 5:38 - His word does not dwell in you because you do not believe

DWELL (continued)
Meditating
Ephesians 3:16-19 - My heart
    Through faith

ENTRANCE
Understanding
Exodus 40:9-16 - Moses was to anoint: altar, utensils, basin, stand, Aaron, and Aaron's sons
Numbers 18:1-4 - Aaron's sons and father's family
    The Levites
    Attend to their duties around the Tabernacle
    Nowhere near the furniture or altar
    They would die
    No

Applying
Leviticus 20:7-8 - To be Holy
    God
Ezekiel 42:20 - Holy from the common
Ezra 9:1 - Because of the detestable practices of the neighboring peoples
2 Corinthians 6:17 - Come out and be separate, touch no unclean thing

Exploring
I Peter 1:16 and Leviticus 11:44 - Be holy because I am holy
Matthew 25:31-32 - Wicked from righteous
    At the end of the age
Romans 8:35-39 - Nothing!

ALTAR
Understanding
Exodus 29:38-41 - Making offerings
Exodus 29:37 - They are made holy

Applying
Psalm 26:6 - In innocence
Psalm 43:4 - With praise
Psalm 118:27 - Festive, joy
Joel 1:13, 2:17 - weeping, mourning
Matthew 5:23-24 - Ask forgiveness from those whom we need to reconcile with

Exploring
Joel 1:13, 2:17 - Prayer for the people
Isaiah 56:7 - Prayer for the nations
Isaiah 6:6-7 - Atonement of sin, forgiveness
Malachi - 1:7-10, 2:13-15 - These things displease God: defiled food; useless fires; unacceptable offerings; flooding altar with meaningless tears; saying that the Lord's table is contemptible; sacrificing blind, crippled animals, unfaithfulness in the marriage vow
Malachi 1:14 - He's cursed

Meditating
Hebrews 13:10 - The cross, where Jesus was the offering
Hebrews 13:12 - We're made holy through His blood

WASH
- *Understanding*
  - Exodus 30:20-21 - So they would not die
  - Numbers 8:6-7 - To be ceremonially purified
- *Applying*
  - Psalm 51:2,7 - yes
  - Acts 22:16 - yes
  - James 4:8 - no
  - Isaiah 1:16-18 - no
  - Isaiah 1:17 - yes
  - Isaiah 1:18 - no
- *Exploring*
  - John 13:5 - their feet
  - John 13:8 - So they could be part of Jesus
  - John 13:10 - To symbolize forgiveness for individual sins
  - Galatians 6:1-2 and John 13:2-15 - We do
  - James 5:16, 19:20 and John 13:2-15 - We do
  - James 5:16 - Through prayer
- *Meditating*
  - Genesis 2:9, 3:22-24 and Revelation 22:14 - The right to the tree of life - to live forever

SACRIFICE
- *Understanding*

Reference	
Job 1:5	D
Exodus 29:38	C
2 Samuel 24:24	A
I Kings 8:62-63	B
Psalm 27:6	C
Psalm 50:14	E
Psalm 54:16	D
Psalm 141:2	A
Ecclesiastes 5:1	B

- *Applying*
  - Isaiah 65:3 - They provoked God
  - Amos 4:5 - They bragged about the offering
  - 2 Chronicles 28:23 - They sacrificed to other gods
  - 2 Kings 3:27 - He sacrificed his son
  - Jonah 2:9 - Salvation comes from the Lord
  - Romans 3:25-26 - Jesus - atonement, justification
  - Romans 8:3-4 - He offered himself for our sins
- *Exploring*
  - I Samuel 15:22 - Burnt offerings and sacrifices with obedience
    - Obedience
  - I Samuel 15:23a - Divination/witchcraft
    - Idolatry

BLOOD
Understanding
- Exodus 29:14 - Sin offering
- Exodus 29:18 - Burnt, pleasing
- Exodus 29:19-21 - The right ear lobe, right thumb and right big toe of Aaron and his sons
    - For their consecration
- Exodus 29:38-43 - lamb, grain, drink

Applying
- Leviticus 1:3 - That it be without defect
    - At the tent of meeting
- Leviticus 1:4 - Laying their hand on the animals head
- Hebrews 10:1 - perfect
- Hebrews 10:4 - take away
- Hebrews 10:12 - Jesus Christ
- Romans 5:9 - His blood
- Ephesians 1:7 - The forgiveness of sins

Exploring
- Hebrews 9:12 - His own blood
- Hebrews 9:13 - Outward, ceremonial
- Hebrews 9:14 - Our consciences
- Hebrews 9:22 - Forgiveness
- Hebrews 10:29 - Punishment

HOLY PLACE
Understanding
- Exodus 29:29-35 - A-F are all verified by the verses
- Exodus 40:4-5 - Table, curtain, lampstand and altar of incense
- Exodus 25:29-30 - Plates, dishes, pitchers, bowls, bread of presence
- Exodus 27:20-21 - Continually from evening till morning
- Exodus 30:7-8 - Every morning and evening

Applying
- Psalm 24:3-4 - He who has clean hands and a pure heart
- Isaiah 63:18 - God's enemies

Some things that can trample the holiness in our sanctuaries: hidden agendas; improper clothing; power struggles; lustful hearts; mixed philosophies and theologies; New Age beliefs; anything that takes our focus away from worship.

Exploring
- Isaiah 57:15 - 1) A high and holy place   2) With him who is contrite
- Isaiah 57:15, I Peter 1:16 - It implies that we must be holy and humble

Meditating
- Micah 6:8 - Reflecting on these qualities will help you prepare for worship by cleansing your heart first and checking your motives.

LAMPSTAND
Understanding
- Exodus 25:37 - seven, light
- Exodus 27:21 - evening, morning
- Exodus 40:4-5 - incense, table

Applying
- Psalm 18:28 - Turns it into light
- Psalm 119:105 - Lights the path
  - God's Word
- Proverbs 6:23 - Commands, teaching
  - Life
- Proverbs 20:27 - Searches man's inmost being
- I Samuel 3:1-4 - speaking

Exploring
- Luke 8:16 - To give light
  - Those who come in
  - None
- Luke 11:34-36 - By letting in light or darkness
  - Good and evil
  - By directing our eyes
- Luke 15:8 - To search for the lost coin
  - c) - lost souls

Meditating
- Revelation 2:4-5 - We have forsaken our first love and not done the things we did at first

LIGHT
Understanding
- Psalm 19:8 - God's precepts and commands
- Psalm 78:14 - Guide them
- Psalm 89:15 - Walk
- Job 33:28 - To the pit
- Isaiah 42:6 an Luke 2:32 - Gentiles and Israel
- I John 1:5 - Light
- John 8:12 - The light of the world

Applying
John 8:12	B
John 5:33-35	B
Matt 5:14	C
Psalm 119:130	A
Proverbs 6:20	C
Proverbs 6:22	A
Proverbs 6:23	B

Exploring
- John 9:5 - Jesus / While He is in the world
- Matthew 28:19-20 - The disciples, us
- Acts 1:8 - Witnesses
- 2 Corinthians 5:14-15 - Christ
- Acts 13:47 - Us, as believers
- Colossians 1:12 - God qualified us to share in the inheritance
- Acts 26:18 - eyes, forgiveness, sanctification

LIGHT (continued)
Meditating
  Isaiah 58:8 1) healing quickly appears
          2) righteousness goes before you
          3) the Lord is your rear guard
  Isaiah 60:1 - The glory of the Lord
  Isaiah 60:3 - Nations and Kings

BREAD
Understanding
1	E
2	B
3	D
4	F
5	C
6	A

Applying
  Job 23:12 - God's words
  Psalm 37:25 - The righteousness
  Proverbs 30:8 - Only what he needs daily
  Isaiah 33:15-16 Walks righteously
         Speaks what is right
         Rejects extortion
         Doesn't plot evil
  Matthew 4:4   The Word of God
  Matthew 6:11   Daily / No

Exploring
  John 6:26 - To get filled with bread
  John 6:27 - Food that endures to eternal life
  John 6:31 - Manna - bread from heaven
  John 6:32:35 - The Father, Jesus
  John 6:50-51 - They'll live forever
    b) spiritual bread

Meditating
  I Corinthians 11:23 - 26
    Jesus' body
    Death
    Jesus' blood
  I Corinthians 11:27-32 - Taking communion improperly

INCENSE
Understanding

Exodus 30: 7-9	1	T	
	2	T	
	3	F	
	4	F	
Exodus 30:34-38	1	T	
	2	F	
	3	F	
Leviticus 16:12-13	True		
Leviticus 24:5-7	False		

INCENSE (continued)
Applying
Psalm 141:2 - Prayer
Proverbs 27:9 - God's
Exodus 30:7-8 - Morning, evening
Leviticus 24:5-9 - Thanks
Revelation 5:8 - bowls, incense, saints
Revelation 8:4 - God

Exploring
2 Chronicles 26:18 - The priests - descendents of Aaron
2 Kings 23:5 - The pagan priests
    Burned incense to Baal, sun, moon, stars, etc...
Exodus 30:34-38 - They should be cut off from the people
Jeremiah 1:16 and 7:9 - pronounce judgement
Jeremiah 11:12 - No help when disaster strikes

Meditating
Malachi 1:11 - Everywhere
    Among the nations

CURTAIN
Understanding
Leviticus 16:2 - death
    because God appeared in the cloud over the atonement cover
Exodus 33:20 - No one was to see the God's face and live
Leviticus 16:11-17 - The smoke would conceal the atonement cover
    Atone for Israel's sin
    No one

Applying
Numbers 4:4-6, 9
    C   B   B   They cannot
Numbers 4:17-20
    B   C   A

Exploring
Matthew 27:50-51 - It was torn from top to bottom
    God did it

Meditating
2 Corinthians 4:3-4   Gospel
    The perishing
    The god of this age
John 12:31 and 14:30 - Satan

MOST HOLY PLACE
Understanding
Exodus 26:34 - Ark of the Testimony
Leviticus 16:2 - No - Because God appeared there
Leviticus 16:16-17 - To make atonement for sins
Leviticus 16:16 - In the midst of their uncleanness
Leviticus 16:17 - Yes, Yes

Applying
1) C   5) F
2) E   6) B
3) H   7) A
4) G   8) D

MOST HOLY PLACE (continued)
Exploring
Romans 3:22-26
1 - Jesus Christ
2 - We are justified
3 - By faith in Jesus
4 - For all have sinned and fell short
Meditating
Hebrews 10:19-20 - Allows us to enter
    With confidence

PRIESTS
Understanding
Exodus 28:1-5 - Aaron and his sons
    To give them dignity and honor
    Skilled men
    From God - He gave them wisdom
Garments that were made: breastpiece, ephod, tunic, turban, robe, sash
Garments specially made for Aaron and his sons: tunics, sashes, headbands
    linen undergarments
Leviticus 21:10 - The High Priest
Leviticus 16:15-17 - Make atonement for himself, his household and community
Hebrews 5:1 - To represent men before God and to offer gifts and sacrifices
Applying
Hebrews 5:4 - No, he must be called by God
Hebrews 5:5-6 - Jesus
Hebrews 7:16 - Power of an indestructible life
Hebrews 7:18-19 - Weak and useless
Hebrews 7:19 - Better hope
Exploring
Hebrews 7:23-24 - It is permanent/forever
Hebrews 7:25 - To intercede
    To pray - to go before God
    He is able to save those who come to God
Hebrews 7:26 - Holy, blameless, set apart from sinners, exalted above the heavens
Hebrews 7:27 - Only offered Himself once - no need for daily sacrifices.
Additional Thoughts
1) God speaks through His Holy Spirit.
2) Always be prepared to give an answer for the hope that is in you. Preach the Word in season and out of season.
3) Revelation and words of knowledge.

COVENANT
Understanding
Exodus 34:28 - The Ten Commandments
Exodus 24:3-8 - The Lord's words and laws
    They agree to obey it all
Genesis 12:1-3 - Great nation
    Bless those who bless him/curse those who curse him
    All the peoples of the earth

COVENANT (continued)
Applying
- Deuteronomy 29:1 - God and the Israelites
- Deuteronomy 29:9 - Carefully obey all
- Deuteronomy 29:12 - An oath
- Deuteronomy 29:13 - To be their God
- Deuteronomy 29:14-15 - All
- Deuteronomy 29:9 - Not following everything God said to do
- Deuteronomy 29:19 - Taking the blessing on himself but going his own way instead of obeying
- Deuteronomy 29:24-25 - They have abandoned the covenant with God
- Hosea 6:7 - By being unfaithful to God
- Malachi 2:8-10 - Breaking faith with one another

Exploring
- Matthew 26:28 - Jesus - by His blood, death
- Acts 3:25 - Yes
- Galatians 3:17 - Confirms it

Meditating
- Hebrews 8:6-10 - It is founded on better promises
    - Write it on our hearts and minds
- Matthew 26:28 - His blood was poured out for the forgiveness of sins
- Hebrews 10:29-31 - Severe punishment - dreadful experience in the hands of the living God

PRESENCE
Understanding
- Genesis 2:15-25, 3:8 - talk with Him, see Him, walk with Him
- Genesis 3:6-7, 10-11, 23-24 - Eating the fruit
    - Result of disobedience-all things listed
- Genesis 4:8-16 - All statements are false
- Deuteronomy 4:37-39 - God's presence, Drive out nations before them, No one
- Exodus 19:16-25 - Up on the mountain, Aaron, No

Applying
- Exodus 33:7-17 - Joshua
    - At the entrance to their tents
    - They did not - they stayed in their tents
    - The priests approach God but the people stay at their tents
    - The priest or minister leads the service as if he is approaching God, while the congregation stays at a distance in their seats.
    - Go with them
    - That if God did not go with them, they didn't want to go
- Exodus 34:29-35 - Covers, hides, keeps secrets
    - It should be completely honest, face to face, with nothing between us and God

Exploring
- Exodus 25:30 - Bread of the presence
    - The presence of God
    - That it would be pleasing, enjoyable
- Job 1:12 - Satan
- Isaiah 63:9 - Angels

Meditating
- Hebrews 9:24 - To appear to God for us